EASY READING INFORMATION SERIES

BUTTER

Written by O. B. Gregory
Illustrated by Denis Wrigley

© 1981 Rourke Publications
1975 O. B. Gregory

Library of Congress Cataloging in Publication Data

Gregory, O. B. (Olive Barnes), 1940-
    Butter.

    (Easy reading information series)
    Summary: Describes how cream is separated
from milk and churned into butter to spread
on bread. Includes questions and vocabulary.
    1. Butter—Juvenile literature.   [1. Butter]
I. Wrigley, Denis, ill.   II. Title.   III. Series.
SF263.G78   637'.2   81-11856
ISBN 0-86625-160-X   AACR2

ROURKE PUBLICATIONS, INC.
Windermere, Fla. 32786

BUTTER

Butter is a food.

We spread it on pieces of bread.

It is used for making cakes.

It can also be used
in all kinds of cooking.

This is the story
of how butter is made.

Butter is made from milk.

The milk comes from cows.

Cows are kept on farms.

They are milked twice a day.

The milk is poured into churns.

A truck goes to the farms
to get the churns.

The churns are taken to the place
where butter is made.

First of all, the milk is weighed.

It is weighed to see how heavy it is.

Then it is tested.

It is tested to see how good it is.

Look at the picture.

There you can see a man
weighing the milk.

He empties the churns
into a machine.

The machine weighs the milk.

Next, the cream is taken
out of the milk.

First of all, the milk is heated.

This makes it easier
to get the cream out.

After the milk has been heated
it is put into another machine.

This machine goes around and around
very quickly.

As the machine goes around,
the cream goes to the middle.

The cream is then taken out.

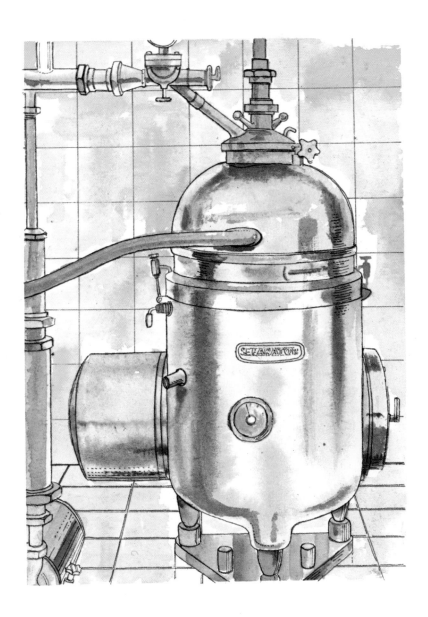

The cream is then pumped
into another machine.

Here the cream is heated.

The cream is heated
to make it safe to eat.

It also helps the cream
to keep for a longer time.

After the cream has been heated
it must be cooled.

This is the sort of cream
which people eat as a topping.

Now we shall see how the cream
is made into butter.

The cream is taken to the factory
where the butter is made.

It is put in a tank.

It is kept in the tank
for about twelve hours.

This makes the cream
begin to go solid.

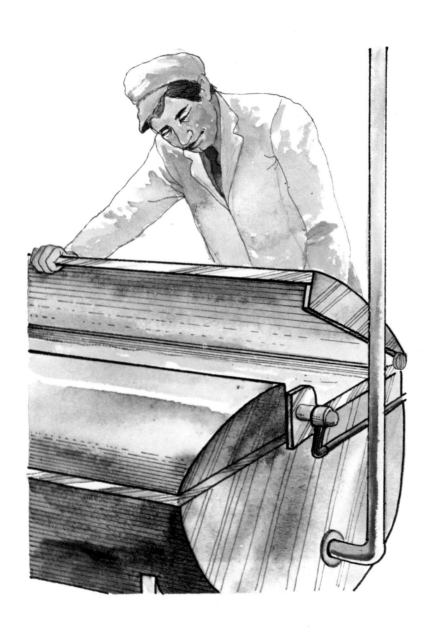

The cream then goes into
a big churn.

Old style churns were made of wood.
Today we use metal.

It is half filled with cream
and then turned
around and around.

There are rollers inside the churn
which help to stir the cream.

After about half an hour
the cream begins to turn
into butter.

At first, small pieces of butter
  float about in thin buttermilk.

The buttermilk is drained off
  and the churn is turned
  around again.

This makes the small pieces of butter
  stick together in big lumps.

The churn door is then opened
  and a container is pushed inside.

The butter falls onto the container
  which is then pulled out again.

The butter is now put into packets,
ready to be sold in the store.

The work is done by machine.

The machine presses the butter
so that each piece is quite solid.

This helps the butter to keep fresh.

Butter is packed in large containers
and shipped to central markets.
There it is packaged into the
size containers you see
in supermarkets.

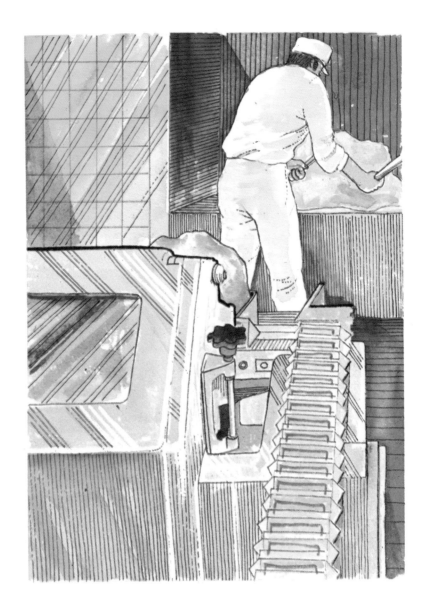

Some countries do not use
        wooden churns. They use stainless
        steel churns.

The churns are turned
        around and around
        just like the wooden churns.

Sometimes the butter is lifted
        out of the churns. Sometimes it is
        pumped from the churn to the
        packing machine.

Wisconsin is one of our most
        important dairy states.

THINGS TO WRITE

1. What is butter made from? (4)

2. Where does the milk
   come from? (4)

3. Where are cows kept? (4)

4. How often are the cows milked? (4)

5. Why is the milk weighed? (6)

6. Why is the milk tested? (6)

7. Why is the milk heated? (8)

8. What does the machine do? (8)

9. Why is the cream heated? (10)

10. How long is the cream kept
    in the tank? (12)

11. What is the churn made of? (14)

12. Where are the rollers? (14)

13. What do the rollers do? (14)

14. What happens after half an
    hour? (14)

15. What happens to the butter-
    milk? (16)

16. What is pushed inside the
    churn? (16)

17. What does the butter do? (16)

18. How is butter put into packets? (18)

19. What is one of our most
    important dairy states? (20)

VOCABULARY

MILK — a white liquid which is drunk by babies and children. It comes from cows, goats and other animals.

CHURN — a large vessel where milk is turned until it becomes butter.

CREAM — the fatty part of milk. When milk is homogenized the milk and cream blend together. When milk is not homogenized the cream rises to the top above the milk.

FACTORY — a building where many people work to produce a certain type of goods.

TEST — the manner in which something is examined to see what it is like, or if it is good.

TANK — a large container which can hold a liquid.

BUTTERMILK — what is left after butter is taken out of cream or milk.

WEIGHT — the amount of heaviness a thing has.